Living through American History

DiscoverRoo
An Imprint of Pop!
popbooksonline.com

Living through WORLD WAR II

by Grace Hansen

WELCOME TO DiscoverRoo!

This book is filled with videos, puzzles, games, and more! Scan the QR codes* while you read, or visit the website below to make this book pop.

popbooksonline.com/world-war-life

abdobooks.com
Published by Pop!, a division of ABDO, PO Box 398166, Minneapolis, Minnesota 55439.

Printed in the United States of America, North Mankato, Minnesota.

052023
092023

THIS BOOK CONTAINS RECYCLED MATERIALS

Cover Photo: Getty Images
Interior Photos: Getty Images
Editor: Elizabeth Andrews
Series Designer: Laura Graphenteen; Neil Klinepier

Library of Congress Control Number: 2022950559

Publisher's Cataloging-in-Publication Data

Names: Hansen, Grace, author.
Title: Living through World War II / by Grace Hansen
Description: Minneapolis, Minnesota : Pop!, 2024 | Series: Living through American history | Includes online resources and index
Identifiers: ISBN 9781098244347 (lib. bdg.) | ISBN 9781098245047 (ebook)
Subjects: LCSH: World War, 1939-1945--Juvenile literature. | World War, 1939-1945--United States--Juvenile literature. | Social history--Juvenile literature.
Classification: DDC 973.2--dc23

*Scanning QR codes requires a web-enabled smart device with a QR code reader app and a camera.

TABLE OF CONTENTS

CHAPTER 1

GOING TO WAR

In the 1930s, the United States was a gloomy place. Many people were out of work because of the Great Depression. Most barely made enough money to survive. Life was too difficult to pay much attention to what was happening in other parts of the world.

WATCH A VIDEO HERE!

The Boy Scouts of America donated their time and effort during the Great Depression and World War II.

A meeting of the Axis powers in Germany in February of 1932 included dictators Benito Mussolini (left) *of Italy and Adolf Hitler* (right) *of Germany.*

Meanwhile, the small island country of Japan was overpopulated. Its resources were limited compared to countries such as the United States and Great Britain. Many Japanese people were struggling. Japan wanted to take more land and increase its resources by force. In 1937, Japan invaded China.

At about the same time in Europe, German **dictator** Adolf Hitler took over Austria and Czechoslovakia. Then in 1939, Hitler and his troops invaded Poland. War broke out across Europe. Soon, Japan joined forces with Germany, Italy, and four other countries to form the Axis powers.

Most people in the United States did not want to be part of another war. World War I (1914–1918) had taken many US lives. Americans did not want more people to die defending countries so far away. However, everything changed on Sunday,

Some Americans believed the United States had good reason to join World War II even before the attack on Pearl Harbor.

BOMBERS RAID MANILA

New York Journal American

No. 19,707—DAILY MONDAY, DECEMBER 8, 1941

7TH SPORT WALL ST. CLOSING

U.S. DECLARES WAR ON JAPAN

President Franklin D. Roosevelt led the nation through two of the greatest crises in its history: the Great Depression and World War II.

December 7, 1941. Japanese forces attacked Pearl Harbor, a US naval base in Hawaii.

CHAPTER 2

BACK TO WORK

Even before the attack on Pearl Harbor, the United States had been sending war materials to support the **Allied powers**. Factories were built or reopened from World War I. The factories made airplanes, tanks, warships, trucks, and

LEARN MORE HERE!

weapons. The demand for these war supplies created many new jobs that were greatly needed.

A worker manufacturing torpedoes at the Washington Navy Yard in 1939.

In 1941, fewer than 500,000 Americans were serving in the armed forces. By 1945, that number had risen to more than 16 million. With so many men serving in the military, factories had no workers. For the first time in years, there was a labor shortage.

American women stepped up to help the nation. Before the war, most middle- and upper-class women were expected to stay home and take care of their families. Money was scarce for women in lower-class and **minority** families. They often had jobs outside of the home but were paid very little.

Women took the place of men at many weapon and ammunition factories to help the war effort.

A factory worker in Nashville, Tennessee, drills rivets into a Vultee A-31 Vengeance dive bomber.

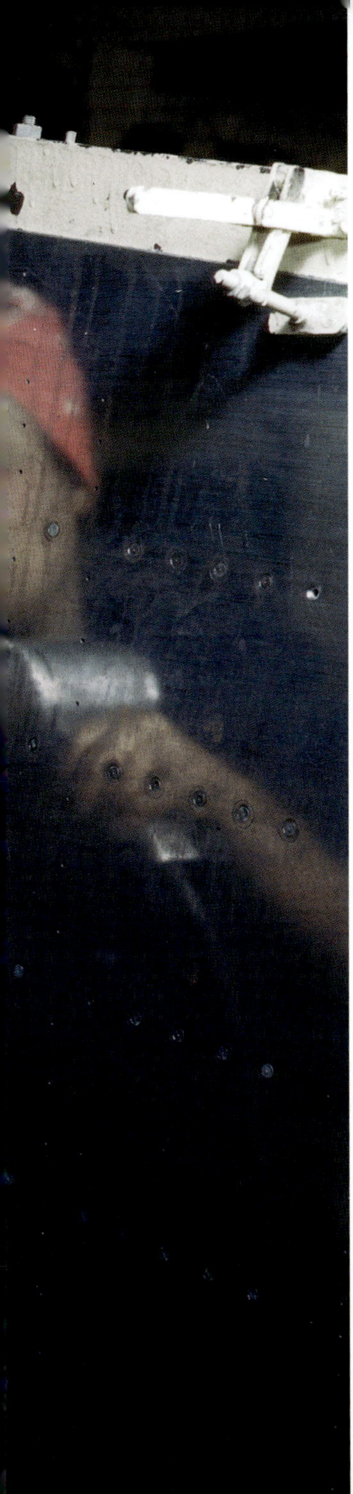

Around 3 million women worked in factories as welders, riveters, and electricians. They built airplanes, ships, and other materials throughout the war. After the war, many women went back to being homemakers. But others fought to keep their jobs in factories. They had proven themselves to be able to do the same jobs as men.

The last names on this government campaign poster represent people of different backgrounds, including Jewish and Italian.

The labor shortage also created better job opportunities for Black Americans. Many moved to cities in the north and west for war-related work. Unfortunately, Black Americans still faced racism and **discrimination** from employers. Some were even met with violence. President Franklin D. Roosevelt issued an executive order that was dated June 25, 1941. It banned discrimination in government and defense jobs. It was a step in the right direction. However, it was not as effective as people hoped.

JAPANESE AMERICANS

After the attack on Pearl Harbor, more than 110,000 Japanese people living in the United States were forced to leave their homes and live in relocation camps. Many of them were American citizens. The camps were made up of buildings surrounded by fences and armed guards. Most lived in the camps for three years or more.

CHAPTER 3

SCHOOL AND PLAY

For most children during the war, school went on as usual. But students were encouraged to find ways to volunteer. They collected scrap metal, old rubber, cooking fats, and old newspapers. These were used for making bullets and other

EXPLORE LINKS HERE!

Children drop off cooking fat at a fat-collection station. Fat was used to make explosives.

war materials. And at least part of each school day was spent discussing war news or other patriotic topics.

DID YOU KNOW?

The labor shortage caused many teenagers to leave high school and join the workforce.

Throughout the war, toys were usually made of wood, paper, or certain kinds of cloth. These items weren't needed for war supplies. For birthdays and holidays, children might get a paper doll, wooden toys, or puzzles. Children also had fun in the neighborhood. They played games such as hide-and-seek, hopscotch, four square, and marbles.

Felt and wood were good materials to make toys with. Neither of these items were rationed during the war.

CHAPTER 4

EFFORT FROM EVERYONE

Doing whatever people could to help the war effort became a way of life. People donated items they did not want or need. They also **rationed** food. In 1942, the government created a program that set limits on the amount of gas, food, and clothing people could buy. There were 20 items that could only be bought with

COMPLETE AN ACTIVITY HERE!

government-issued stamps. These were like coupons. People were only allowed to buy rationed items, such as sugar, coffee, and canned goods, if they had the right stamp.

A sixth grade teacher shows her students how to use a war ration book.

Victory gardens were an inexpensive way for Americans to support their country.

Many Americans started home gardens named victory gardens. People grew vegetables, fruits, and herbs. More than 20 million victory gardens throughout the US provided about 40% of the produce eaten by Americans.

People also invested in the war by buying **savings bonds**. These bonds helped the government raise money to pay soldiers and make war materials.

One of many posters created by the US government during the war effort.

Entertainers did their part too. Music, comedy, and dramatic radio programs entertained eager listeners. People also tuned in to hear famous news anchors Walter Winchell or Edward R. Murrow report the latest war news.

Between 1942 and 1946, nearly 60 million people went to the movies each week. Movies

Hollywood actress Lana Turner promotes the purchasing of war bonds in June of 1942.

were an escape from the **sacrifices** of wartime. The average cost of a movie ticket was 27 cents. This bought moviegoers a newsreel, a cartoon, and the main feature.

World War II touched the lives of every American and changed the nation. Everyone understood the importance of working together to help the war effort. The United States became a world leader in producing weapons, food, and supplies. People's **resourcefulness** helped shorten the war. The nation was rewarded with an economic boom in the years that followed.

A DAY IN THE LIFE

Sally lives with her family near Saint Louis, Missouri. Her father is away serving in the US Navy. Sally's mom now works in a factory. Sally helps out at home.

6:00 AM

Sally wakes up and gets dressed for school. She wakes her younger brothers and helps them get ready for school too.

7:00 AM

Sally makes lunches for the whole family while her mother cooks breakfast. Her mother leaves to catch the bus for her job at the factory. Sally cleans the kitchen before she and the boys walk to school.

3:30 PM

Sally and her brothers walk home from school. They sit down at the table to do their homework. Then they all tend the victory garden in the backyard. Sally picks carrots and potatoes. The boys pull weeds.

5:30 PM

Sally starts dinner. She slices the carrots and potatoes and puts them in a pot with a small amount of water, butter, and salt. She is sure not to waste any butter, since it is a **rationed** item.

7:30 PM

Sally walks to her friend Laura's house. Laura's mother is the Girl Scout leader. Tonight they are going to roll bandages and make care packages for the soldiers.

9:00 PM

Sally arrives home in time to listen to the *Kraft Music Hall* radio program with her mother before bed.

MAKING CONNECTIONS

TEXT-TO-SELF

How might your life have looked if you lived during World War II? What would your daily tasks include?

TEXT-TO-TEXT

Have you read any other books about life during World War II? Did you learn anything new from those books?

TEXT-TO-WORLD

The United States was not the only country where life changed a lot during World War II. Can you think of any other countries where people's lives were greatly impacted due to the war?

GLOSSARY

Allied powers — a group of nations that formed during World War II to oppose the Axis powers. The main members in 1941 were the United Kingdom, the United States, the Soviet Union, and China.

dictator — a ruler who has total authority.

discrimination — the unjust treatment of certain groups of people based on characteristics such as race, gender, religion, etc.

minority — a group of people in a country who make up a smaller part of the whole population.

ration — a fixed share or portion.

resourceful — capable of dealing with difficult situations quickly and imaginatively.

sacrifice — the act of giving up something of value.

savings bond — a bond issued by the government and sold to the general public. A bond is a piece of paper that the government gives when it borrows money. It promises to repay the money along with interest.

INDEX